A Midsummer Night's Dream

William Shakespeare

Abridged and adapted by Mark Falstein

Illustrated by Karen Loccisano

A PACEMAKER CLASSIC

GLOBE FEARON
EDUCATIONAL PUBLISHER
Upper Saddle River, New Jersey
www.globefearon.com

Executive Editor: Joan Carrafiello
Project Editor: Karen Bernhaut
Editorial Assistant: Keisha Carter
Production Director: Penny Gibson
Print Buyer: Cheryl Johnson
Production Editor: Alan Dalgleish
Desktop Specialist: Margarita T. Linnartz
Art Direction: Joan Jacobus
Marketing Manager: Marge Curson
Cover and Interior Illustrations: Karen Loccisano
Cover Design: Margarita T. Linnartz

Printed in the United States of America
2 3 4 5 6 7 8 9 10   99

ISBN 0-835-91407-0

GLOBE FEARON EDUCATIONAL PUBLISHER
Upper Saddle River, New Jersey
www.globefearon.com

Contents

Cast of Characters

THESEUS	Duke of Athens
HIPPOLYTA	Queen of the Amazons
EGEUS	An Athenian citizen
HERMIA	Egeus's daughter
LYSANDER	A young man in love with Hermia
DEMETRIUS	Another man in love with Hermia
HELENA	Hermia's friend, who is in love with Demetrius
PETER QUINCE	A carpenter
NICK BOTTOM	A weaver
FRANCIS FLUTE	A bellows-mender
ROBIN STARVELING	A tailor
TOM SNOUT	A tinker (mender of pots and pans)
SNUG	A joiner (cabinetmaker)
PUCK (Robin Goodfellow)	A mischievous sprite; a fairy
OBERON	King of the fairies
TITANIA	Queen of the fairies
PEASEBLOSSOM, COBWEB, MOTE, AND MUSTARDSEED	Four fairies who serve Titania
PHILOSTRATE	Theseus's servant

Act 1

*The play takes place long ago in Greece.
Theseus, duke of Athens, is planning his wedding
with Hippolyta. She is the queen of the Amazons,
a tribe of warrior women. Egeus appears with
his daughter, Hermia. He wants Theseus to force
Hermia to marry Demetrius, the man he has cho-
sen for her. But Hermia loves another man,
Lysander. She and Lysander decide to run away
together. They tell their plan to Hermia's friend,
Helena. She is in love with Demetrius. To win
his favor, Helena tells him what Hermia and
Lysander plan to do.*

*In another part of Athens, six working men
meet. They are planning to put on a play at
Theseus and Hippolyta's wedding. Their leader is
Peter Quince, a carpenter. Nick Bottom, a
weaver, wants to play all the parts himself.*

Scene 1

Theseus's palace. THESEUS *and* HIPPOLYTA *enter,
with* SERVANTS.

THESEUS: Fair Hippolyta, our wedding day
    Draws near. Four happy days bring in
    Another moon. But oh, I think, how slowly
    The old moon goes! She holds back my wants
    Like an old widow holds a young man's money
    Left to him by his father.

HIPPOLYTA: Four days will quickly turn to night.
    Four nights will quickly dream away the time.
    And then the new moon, like a silver bow,
    Will shine upon our wedding.

1

THESEUS: Hippolyta, I won you with my sword.
I earned your love by wounding you in war.
But I will wed you in a different way:
With fine food, dancing, and good times!

(EGEUS, HERMIA, LYSANDER, *and* DEMETRIUS *enter.*)

EGEUS: Happy be Theseus, our great duke!

THESEUS: Thanks, good Egeus. What's your news?

EGEUS: Trouble with my daughter Hermia!
Step up, Demetrius. This man has my consent
To marry her. Now you, Lysander. This man
Has made her fall in love with him!
He has used all the tricks young men know
That work on girls her age.
And so he has stolen my daughter's heart.
He has turned her away from me, her father.
She no longer obeys me. She will not
Consent to marry Demetrius.
And so, my lord, I ask you for my right.
As she is mine, I may give her away
To the man I choose or send her
To her death. You know that is our law.

THESEUS: What do you say, Hermia? Remember:
Your father should be like a god to you.
He formed your beauty. You are just a copy
He has printed, as in wax. He has the right
To leave the copy or to melt it down.
Demetrius is a good man.

HERMIA: So is Lysander.

THESEUS: In himself he is. But in this case,
Because of your father's opinion,
The other must be found the better man.

HERMIA: I wish my father saw it with my eyes.

THESEUS: It's your eyes that must look at it his
    way.

HERMIA: I beg you, lord, to pardon me.
    I do not know what power makes me bold.
    I do not know if it is right for me
    To stand before you telling you my thoughts.
    But I must ask you, lord, so I may know:
    What is the worst that may be done to me
    If I refuse to wed Demetrius?

THESEUS: Either to die or never wed at all.
    And so, Hermia, look inside yourself.
    Look at your feelings. Think of your youth.
    Would you be happy as a childless nun,
    Singing songs to the goddess of the moon?
    That is the life that you will live forever
    If you don't agree to your father's choice.

HERMIA: So will I live—and die, my lord.
    This I will do before I give my life
    To one I do not love.

THESEUS: Take time to think.
    On the new moon, be ready to die
    If you won't give in to your father's will
    And wed Demetrius. Or else, be sure
    That you'll forever live your life alone.

DEMETRIUS: Give in, Hermia.
    You, too, Lysander.
    Give up your claim to what is rightly mine.

LYSANDER: Let me have Hermia's love.
    You have her father's. Go and marry him.

EGEUS: Yes, Lysander, he does have my love.
And so my love will give him what is mine.

LYSANDER (*to* THESEUS): My lord, I am as good a
man as he.
In every way, I'm equal to Demetrius.
In some ways I'm better. But leave such talk
Aside. Hermia loves me. That's what counts.
And so why shouldn't I return her love?
Demetrius courted Nedar's daughter, Helena,
And won her soul. Now that sweet lady is
In love with him, and he chases Hermia.

THESEUS: I've heard about that, and I meant
To speak about it with Demetrius.
But being so busy with my wedding plans,
I did forget it. But come, Demetrius.
You too, Egeus. Both of you, come with me.
I must have a private word with you.
For you, fair Hermia, you have four days
To fit your wishes to your father's will.
Or else, you must give in to Athens's law.

(*All but* HERMIA *and* LYSANDER *exit.*)

LYSANDER: Love, why is your face so white?
What happened to the roses that were
there?

HERMIA: They must need rain.
I could well give it to them from my eyes.

LYSANDER: From everything I've heard,
The course of true love never did run smooth.
Either the two were different by wealth—

HERMIA: Oh, no! Rich, and in love with poor!

LYSANDER: Or else their ages did not match—

HERMIA: Oh, my! Old, and in love with young!

LYSANDER: Or their friends did not approve—

HERMIA: Oh, awful! To choose love by others' eyes!

LYSANDER: Or, if they were well matched,
  War or sickness put an end to it.
  Love lasts only a moment, like a sound.
  It is as quick as a shadow or a dream.
  Before a person may say "Look at this!"
  The jaws of darkness have eaten it up.

HERMIA: If this is how it always is with love,
  It must be law. So we must be patient
  And take it with our dreams and tears.

LYSANDER: Well said, Hermia. Now, hear me:
  I have a rich aunt who has no children.
  She's always thought of me as her own son.
  Her house is only 20 miles from Athens.
  There, sweet Hermia, I may marry you,
  And there the laws of Athens cannot follow.
  If you love me, slip out of your house
  Tomorrow night and meet me in the woods
  A mile outside the town.

HERMIA: My good Lysander,
  I swear to you by Cupid's strongest bow.
  I swear by all the promises men have broken
  (Which are more than women ever made).
  Tomorrow night I'll truly meet you there.

LYSANDER: Keep that promise, love.
  Look, here comes Helena.

(HELENA *enters.*)

HERMIA: Hello, fair Helena.

HELENA: You call me "fair?"
Demetrius loves your "fairness." Lucky you!
Your eyes like stars, your voice so sweet!
Sickness is catching. If beauty were so,
I'd catch yours, fair Hermia, before I go.
Teach me how you look, and with what art
You lead the dancing of Demetrius's heart!

HERMIA: I frown upon him; yet he loves me still.

HELENA: I wish your frowns would teach my
smiles such skill!

HERMIA: The more I hate, the more he follows me.

HELENA: The more I love, the more he hates me.

HERMIA: He's a fool, Helena. It's not my fault.

HELENA: It's your beauty. I wish I had that fault.

HERMIA: Be happy. He won't see me again.
Lysander and I are going away from here.

LYSANDER: Helena, we'll tell you our plan:
Tomorrow night, when the moon sees her face
In the watery mirror, we will steal away.

HERMIA: You know the wood where you and I
Would lie upon the grass when we were young
And tell each other our most secret thoughts?
That's where we'll meet. Lysander and I
Will turn our eyes away from Athens.
We'll meet new people and make new friends.
Good-bye, childhood playmate! Pray for us,
And may good luck bring you Demetrius.

Lysander, dear, we must keep out of sight
Of one another till tomorrow night!

LYSANDER: Good-bye, my Hermia.
(HERMIA *exits.*) Helena, you too,
And as you love Demetrius, may he love you!

(LYSANDER *exits.*)

HELENA: Happier some people are than others!
In Athens, I am thought as fair as she.
But what of it? Demetrius does not think so.
And as he looks on Hermia, so I
Love everything about him. Love can change
A person's worst faults to something fine.
Love sees not with the eyes, but with the mind.
That's why Cupid is always painted blind.
He does not think; he never has a worry.
Wings, but no eyes: blind, and in a hurry.
And that's why love is said to be a child:
Because his choices are so often wild.
Love often lies. Demetrius loved me once.
He swore to me that he was only mine.
That was before he looked on Hermia's eyes.
I will go and tell him of her plan.
Then he will follow her tomorrow night.
Maybe he will thank me for this news.
If that is so, I will not mind the pain,
For it may bring him back to me again.

(HELENA *exits.*)

Scene 2

Peter Quince's house. QUINCE, SNUG, BOTTOM,
FLUTE, SNOUT, *and* STARVELING *enter.*

QUINCE: Is our group all here?

BOTTOM: You had better call them all together, following your list.

QUINCE: Here is the list of every man in Athens who is fit to act in a play. We will put on this play for the duke and duchess at their wedding.

BOTTOM: First, good Peter Quince, say what the play is about. Then read the names of the actors. That way you grow to a point.

QUINCE: Our play is "The most sad comedy and most cruel death of Pyramus and Thisbe."

BOTTOM: A very good piece of work and fun. Now, good Peter Quince, call your list of actors. Masters, spread yourselves.

QUINCE: Answer as I call you. Nick Bottom, the weaver.

BOTTOM: Ready. Name my part, and go on.

QUINCE: You, Nick Bottom, are set down for Pyramus.

BOTTOM: What is Pyramus—a lover or a hero?

QUINCE: A man who kills himself for love.

BOTTOM: That will ask some tears. If I do it, let the audience take care of their eyes. I will move storms! I will make them all sorry for me! Yet I'd rather be a hero. I could play Hercules well. That's a part to tear a cat in! A high thing! A lover is more pitiful. Now name the other players.

QUINCE: Francis Flute, the bellows-mender.

FLUTE: Here, Peter Quince!

QUINCE: You must play Thisbe.

FLUTE: What is Thisbe? A knight?

QUINCE: She is the lady Pyramus must love.

FLUTE: Let me not play a woman. I'm growing a beard.

QUINCE: That's all right. You'll wear a mask, and speak as small as you want.

BOTTOM: Let me play Thisbe, too. I'll speak in a hugely little voice: "Thisbe, Thisbe!" "Ah Pyramus, my dear love! Your Thisbe dear and lady dear—"

QUINCE: No, you're Pyramus, and Flute, you're Thisbe.

BOTTOM: Well, go on.

QUINCE: Robin Starveling, the tailor.

STARVELING: Here, Peter Quince.

QUINCE: You must play Thisbe's mother. Tom Snout, the tinker.

SNOUT: Here, Peter Quince.

QUINCE: You, Pyramus's father. I'll be Thisbe's father. And Snug, the joiner, you play the lion.

SNUG: Have you the lion's part written? Please, give it to me now. I learn slowly.

QUINCE: You may play it as you wish. It is nothing but roaring.

BOTTOM: Let me play the lion, too. My roar will do any man's heart good. I will roar so terribly that the duke will say, "Let him roar again! Let him roar again!"

QUINCE: And the duchess and all the ladies will scream. That would be enough to hang us all.

BOTTOM: It's true, friends. If we scare the ladies, they will have reason to hang us. But I will roar as sweetly as a lamb.

QUINCE: You can play no part but Pyramus, as sweet a man as you could ever meet. He is a true gentleman. Who else but you could play the part? (*Giving out the parts*) Masters, here are your parts. I beg you and plead with you to learn them by tomorrow night. We'll meet in the wood a mile outside of town. We'll rehearse by moonlight. If we meet in the city, we will be dogged with company. Everyone will know what we are up to. I hope you won't let me down.

BOTTOM: We will meet, and we will rehearse, and we will be perfect.

(*They exit.*)

Act 2

*In the woods, Oberon, the fairy king, quarrels
with his queen, Titania. He decides to play a
trick on her. He tells Puck, a mischievous sprite,
to get him a magic flower. He will put juice from
this flower on Titania's eyes while she sleeps.
This will make her fall in love with the next
living thing she sees.*

*Demetrius appears and looks for Hermia.
Helena follows him, begging for his love.
Oberon feels sorry for her. He tells Puck to put
some of the flower juice on the eyes of a young
man wearing Athenian clothes. Puck is to make
sure the next person the man sees is Helena.
Puck follows his order, but he gets the wrong
Athenian.*

Scene 1

The woods. PUCK *and another* FAIRY *enter.*

PUCK: How now, spirit? Where do you wander?

FAIRY: Over hill, over dale,
   Through bush, through brier.
   Over field, over fence,
   Through river, through fire.
   I do wander everywhere,
   Faster than the moon.
   And I serve the fairy queen;
   I make her rings of dew upon the green.
   Good-bye, lively spirit! I must go.
   Our queen and her elves will be here soon.

PUCK: The king gives a party here tonight.

Be careful that the queen stays out of his sight,
For Oberon is angry. The queen has stolen
A boy from a faraway king and taken him
As her servant. Oberon wants the boy
For himself, to serve him as a knight.
But the queen keeps the boy away from him.
She crowns him with flowers. He's her joy.
Now any time they meet, in wood or field,
By clear spring, or under stars of night,
Our king and queen argue over him.

FAIRY: If I'm not wrong, I think I know you.
Are you not that clever, naughty sprite
Called Robin Goodfellow? Are you not he
Who scares the village girls? The one
Who steals cream from milk, leads travelers
The wrong way, plays tricks on everyone?
Are you not the one they call "Sweet Puck?"

PUCK: You have it right.
I am that merry wanderer of the night.
I joke with Oberon and make him smile.
And, yes, it is I who make people jump
With sudden noises. Sometimes I hide
In a bowl of soup and make it spill
On someone's chin. A wise old woman
Sometimes thinks I am a three-legged stool.
I slip from under her, and down she falls!
Then everyone laughs! But make room, fairy.
Here comes Oberon.

FAIRY: And Titania!

(OBERON *enters from one side, with his* FAIRIES.
TITANIA *enters from the other side, with hers.*)

OBERON: Ill met you by moonlight, proud Titania.

TITANIA: What, Oberon? Fairies, let us go.
I'll have nothing of his company.

OBERON: Wait, you. Am I not your husband?

TITANIA: Then I am your wife. But I do know
How you pass your time,
Promising love to all the young girls.
What brings you here? To see Hippolyta,
Your old love, be married to her duke?

OBERON: How can you speak of that, Titania?
I know about your love for Theseus.
Wasn't it you who made him break
So many promises to so many women?

TITANIA: These are jealous lies.
Not once since summer has begun have we
Been free to do our dances with the wind.
You interrupt our fun with angry talk
By spring or rushing stream or sandy beach.
And so the wind whistles for no use.
In revenge, it brings up water from the sea
And floods the land. Fields fill with mud.
Green corn rots in its rows. Sheep die.
The seasons are confused. The human mortals
Want their winter. Summer flowers bloom
On its crown of ice. The world, amazed,
Does not know which is which! And all this
Comes from our arguing. We are its parents.

OBERON: Will you stop, then? It's up to you.
Why should Titania cross her Oberon?
All I ask for is a stolen little boy.

TITANIA: Don't even think about it.
    I would not sell him for all Fairyland!
    His mother made a promise to serve me.
    Often we sat together on the sand.
    We'd watch the ships, their sails pregnant
    With the wind, as she was with that child.
    But, being mortal, she died as he was born.
    It is for her that I raise the boy,
    And for her, I will not part with him.

OBERON: How long will you stay in this wood?

TITANIA: Until after Theseus's wedding day.
    If you will dance with us, come with us.
    If you will not, then stay away from me.

OBERON: Give me the boy, and I will go with you.

TITANIA: Not for the world. Fairies, away.
    There'll be a real fight here if I stay.

(TITANIA *and her* FAIRIES *exit.*)

OBERON: Go, then. You won't leave this wood
    Until I get even for this injury.
    Gentle Puck, come here. There is a flower,
    Milk-white and purple with Cupid's wound.
    Young girls call it "love-in-idleness."
    Get it for me. I showed it to you once.
    The juice of it, laid on sleeping eyes,
    Will make a man or woman fall in love
    With the next live creature that it sees.
    Get me this flower. Then be back here again
    Before a whale can swim three miles.

PUCK: I'll put a girdle round about the earth
    In 40 minutes.

(PUCK *exits.*)

OBERON: When I have this juice,
　　I'll watch Titania as she sleeps
　　And drop it on her eyes. When she wakes,
　　She'll love the next thing that she sees.
　　It might be a lion, bear, wolf, or monkey.
　　Before I take this spell away from her,
　　I'll get that boy. But who comes here?
　　I am invisible, and I will hear them talk.

(DEMETRIUS *enters, with* HELENA *after him.*)

DEMETRIUS: I do not love you. Get away from me!
　　Where is Lysander and fair Hermia?
　　You told me they'd be coming to this wood.
　　Get out of here, and follow me no more!

HELENA: You draw me like a magnet. My heart
　　Is true as steel. Lose your power to draw,
　　And I'll have no power to follow.

DEMETRIUS: Draw you? Haven't I told you?
　　I do not love you!

HELENA: And for that, I love you even more.
　　I am your dog, Demetrius.
　　Beat me, and I shall follow at your feet.
　　Do what you wish. Just let me follow you.

DEMETRIUS: It makes me sick to look at you.

HELENA: I am sick when I don't look at you.

DEMETRIUS: Don't you care what people think?
　　You leave the city and chase after one
　　Who does not love you? You trust the night
　　And this lonely place to keep you safe?

HELENA: Your excellence protects me.
It is not night when I can see your face.
And no place can be lonely with you there,
For you are all the world.

DEMETRIUS: I'll run and hide in the bushes
And leave you to the mercy of wild animals.

HELENA: The wildest has a kinder heart than you.
Run, then. The deer will chase the tiger.

DEMETRIUS: I won't listen to you. Let me go.
Or, if you follow me, do not believe
That I won't do you harm.

HELENA: Yes, you do harm! Your wrongs offend
all women.
We cannot fight for love, as men may do.
We should be wooed, and were not made to woo.
(DEMETRIUS *exits.*)
I'll follow you. I'll make a heaven of hell
If I die by the hand I love so well.

(HELENA *exits.*)

OBERON: Good-bye, sweet thing. Before he
leaves this grove,
You will run, and he will seek your love.
(PUCK *enters.*)
Welcome, wanderer. Do you have the flower?

PUCK: Yes, here it is.

OBERON: Please, give it to me.
(PUCK *gives him the flower.*)
I know a bank where the wild thyme blows,
Where every kind of lovely flower grows.

There Titania often sleeps at night,
Tired out from dances and delight.
There I'll put this juice upon her eyes.
Take some of it and look around this grove.
(*He gives* PUCK *some of the flower.*)
A sweet Athenian lady is in love
With a man who hates her. Paint his eyes.
Be certain that the next thing that he sees
May be the lady. You'll know this young man
By the Athenian clothes that he has on.
Do it with care. Be sure he loves her more
Than she does him.
Meet me here before first rooster crow.

PUCK: Don't worry, lord. I shall make it so.

(*They exit.*)

Scene 2

Another part of the wood. TITANIA *enters with her* FAIRIES.

TITANIA: Come now, a dance and fairy song.
Then, for a while, go away from here.
(*She points to different* FAIRIES.)
You will kill the worms that eat the roses.
You will war with bats, and use their wings
To make coats for my elves. And you, keep back
The noisy owls that come here at night
And hoot at us. Sing me now to sleep.
Then go do your jobs and let me rest.

(TITANIA *lies down. The* FAIRIES *sing.*)

FAIRIES: *Snakes and spiders, come not near.*
Worms and lizards, don't be seen.

Beetles black, away from here.
Come not near our fairy queen.

(TITANIA *sleeps.*)

A FAIRY: All is well. Now, away!

(*The* FAIRIES *exit.* OBERON *enters and places the juice on* TITANIA*'s eyes.*)

OBERON: What you see when you awake,
    As your true love you will take.
    Be sick with love for his sake.
    Be it pig, or cat, or big brown bear,
    Open your eyes, and it is your dear.
    Wake when something vile is near.

(OBERON *exits.* HERMIA *and* LYSANDER *enter.*)

LYSANDER: Dear love, you're weak from wandering
    in the wood.
    And to speak truly, we have lost our way.
    Let's rest, Hermia, if you think it good.
    We'll wait here for the comfort of the day.

HERMIA: I'm with you. Find yourself a bed.
    Here on this bank I will rest my head.

LYSANDER: One spot shall serve as pillow for us
    both.

HERMIA: No, Lysander. For my sake, my dear,
    Do not lie so very near.

LYSANDER: Do not take me wrong, my sweet!
    I mean only that our two hearts are one.
    So, let me make my bedroom by your side.
    For there, Hermia, I have not lied.

HERMIA: You make a very pretty riddle.

Now, forgive my manners and my pride,
If Hermia meant to say Lysander lied.
But, my gentle friend, lie further off.
Such distance, it might well be said,
Is right for an unmarried man and maid.
So stay away—and good night, sweet friend.
And may we love each other till life's end!

LYSANDER: And may my life end if I end love!
Here's my bed. Sleep give you all his rest.

(*They sleep.* PUCK *enters.*)

PUCK: Through the forest I have gone,
But I found no Athenian.
(*He sees* LYSANDER.)
Night and quiet! Who is here?
Clothes of Athens he does wear.
This is the one my master said
Hated the Athenian maid.
And here the maid is, sleeping sound,
On the wet and dirty ground.
(*He puts the juice on* LYSANDER's *eyes.*)
When you wake, let love keep
Your eyes so bright you cannot sleep.
So awake when I am gone.
I must now go to Oberon.

(PUCK *exits.* DEMETRIUS *and* HELENA *enter, running.*)

HELENA: Stay, even if you kill me, love!

DEMETRIUS: Go away. Don't chase me any more.

HELENA: You would leave me here in the dark?

DEMETRIUS: Stay here! I'll go on alone.

(DEMETRIUS *exits.*)

HELENA: Oh, I am out of breath.
　　The more I pray, the less I am answered.
　　Happy is Hermia, with her pretty eyes.
　　How did they get so bright? Not with tears.
　　If so, mine should be prettier than hers.
　　No, no, I am as ugly as a bear.
　　Even animals run from me in fear.
　　But who is here? Lysander, on the ground!
　　Dead, or asleep? I see no blood, no wound.
　　Lysander, if you live, good sir, awake.

LYSANDER (*waking up*): And run through fire for you!
　　Lovely Helena! Now I can see your heart.
　　Where is Demetrius? Oh, that vile word!
　　That name is fit to die upon my sword!

HELENA: Do not say that, Lysander.
　　So what if he loves Hermia? She loves you.
　　Isn't that enough?

LYSANDER: What, Hermia? I'm sorry now
　　For all the boring time I spent with her.
　　I love not Hermia, but Helena!
　　Reason changes a man's heart. I am young,
　　And, until now, my reason's not been ripe.
　　Now reason says you are the lovelier maid.
　　It leads me to your eyes. There I may look,
　　And read love's stories in love's richest book.

HELENA: Why do you make fun of me like this?
　　What did I do that you should treat me so?
　　Is it not enough that I never can
　　Win a sweet look from Demetrius's eye?
　　Why must you do me such a wrong? Good-bye.
　　I must say, I thought you were more kind.

Oh, that a lady one man has refused
Should then be by another abused!

(HELENA *exits.*)

LYSANDER: Hermia, stay there.
Never come near Lysander again.
It is as if I ate too many sweets:
My stomach now is deeply sick of you.
I hate you. I turn my love and might
To Helena, that I may be her knight.

(LYSANDER *exits.* HERMIA *wakes up.*)

HERMIA: Help me, Lysander! Help me!
Oh, get this crawling snake away from me!
Oh! I'm awake now. What a dream I had!
Lysander, look how I shake with fear.
I thought a snake was eating at my heart,
And you sat smiling at him. What, Lysander?
Where are you? Do you hear me? Are you near?
Speak, if you can hear me! Oh, I'm scared!
I'm wide awake now, and you are not here.
I'll either find you soon or die of fear!

(*She exits.*)

Act 3

Bottom and his friends meet to rehearse their play. Puck finds them close to where Titania lies asleep. He sets a donkey's head on Bottom without his knowing. When Titania wakes, she sees Bottom and falls in love with him.

Puck tells Oberon how well his plan is working. When Demetrius enters, chasing Hermia, Oberon realizes Puck's mistake. He tells Puck to find Helena, while he puts the flower juice on Demetrius's eyes himself. Now both Lysander and Demetrius are in love with Helena. She thinks they are making fun of her. Hermia is angry, and Demetrius and Lysander are ready to kill each other. Puck thinks it is all great fun, but Oberon has another flower that will set things right.

Scene 1

The wood. TITANIA *is still asleep onstage. Enter* QUINCE, BOTTOM, SNOUT, STARVELING, SNUG, *and* FLUTE.

BOTTOM: Are we all here?

QUINCE: Yes, and right on time. Here's a perfect place for our rehearsal. This green spot will be our stage, those bushes our dressing room. We will act it out as we will before the duke.

BOTTOM: Peter Quince?

QUINCE: What do you say, Bottom?

BOTTOM: There are things in this comedy of Pyramus and Thisbe that will never do. First, Pyramus must kill himself with a sword. The ladies will not stand for it. What do you say to that?

SNOUT: That's a dangerous fear.

STARVELING: I believe we must leave that part out.

BOTTOM: Not at all! I have a plan. Write a prologue for me to speak. Let it say that we will do no harm with our swords, that Pyramus is not really killed. Say too that I am not Pyramus, but Bottom, the weaver. This will end their fear.

QUINCE: Very well, we will do it.

SNOUT: Won't the ladies be afraid of the lion?

STARVELING: They will, I promise you.

BOTTOM: Masters, it is terrible to bring in a lion among ladies. There is no more fearful a bird than a lion.

SNOUT: Another prologue must say that he is not a lion.

BOTTOM: No, you must name his name, and half his face must show through the lion's neck. And he must say this at some point: "Ladies," or "Fair ladies, I beg you—" No, "I wish you—" No, "I ask you not to be afraid! I am not really a lion. I am a man like any other." And then have him say plainly that he is Snug, the joiner.

QUINCE: All right. But there are still two
problems. First, how do we bring moonlight
into a room? As you know, Pyramus and
Thisbe meet by moonlight.

SNOUT: Will the moon shine the night of our play?

BOTTOM: A calendar, bring me a calendar!

(QUINCE *takes out a calendar.*)

QUINCE: Yes, it will shine that night.

BOTTOM: Well, then, leave a window open in
the room where we perform, and let the
moon shine in.

QUINCE: Yes, and someone can come in dressed
as the Man in the Moon. Now, we must also
have a wall. The story says Pyramus and
Thisbe talked through a hole in a wall.

SNOUT: You can never bring a wall into the
room. What do you say, Bottom?

BOTTOM: One of us must play the wall. And let him
have plaster or mud on him to show he's a
wall. He can hold his fingers like this, and
Pyramus and Thisbe can talk through the hole.

QUINCE: Good, then we're set. Let us rehearse
our parts. Pyramus, you start. When you go
offstage, go into those bushes.

(PUCK *enters, invisible to those onstage.*)

PUCK (*aside*): Who are these clowns
So near where the fairy queen sleeps?
What, a play? I'll be the audience,
And maybe an actor, too.

BOTTOM (*as Pyramus*):
  Thisbe, as sweet as flowers smell,
  So does your breath. But listen!
  A voice! Stay here awhile,
  And soon I will appear to you.

(*He exits, into the bushes.*)

PUCK (*aside*): A stranger Pyramus has never been played.

(*He exits, following* BOTTOM.)

FLUTE: Do I speak now?

QUINCE: Yes, you must. Don't you understand? He's only gone to see a noise he has heard. He's coming right back.

FLUTE (*as Thisbe*):
  My Pyramus, white as a red rose,
  As true as the truest horse,
  I'll meet you, then, at Ninny's tomb.

QUINCE: "Ninus's" tomb. And you don't say that line yet. That's your answer to Pyramus. Pyramus, you must enter. You missed your cue. It is "truest horse."

(PUCK *enters with* BOTTOM, *who wears a donkey's head without realizing it.*)

BOTTOM (*as Pyramus*):
  If I am fair, fair Thisbe, I am yours.

QUINCE (*Frightened by the donkey's head*): Oh, a monster! We are haunted! Run, masters, run! Help!

(QUINCE, FLUTE, SNOUT, SNUG, *and* STARVELING *exit.*)

29

PUCK: I'll follow you. I'll lead in circles.
  I'll follow you through wood and swamp.
  Sometimes I'll be a horse, sometimes a dog.
  I'll be a pig, a bear, sometimes a fire.
  I'll neigh, bark, grunt, roar, burn,
  Like horse, dog, pig, bear, fire at every turn.

(PUCK *exits.*)

BOTTOM: Why did they run away? This is a trick
  to make me afraid. They mean to make a
  donkey of me, but I won't fall for it. I won't
  move from here. I will sing, so they will
  know I am not afraid. (*He sings:*)
  The blackbird, with its orange bill,
  The robin, with its song so true—

TITANIA (*waking up*): What angel moves me
      from my bed of flowers?
  I ask you, gentle mortal, sing again.
  My ear is much delighted with your voice.
  So is my eye a slave to your fine looks.
  Everything about you stirs my feelings
  At my first sight. I swear, I love you.

BOTTOM: I think, lady, you have little reason for
  that. But to tell the truth, reason and love
  are not good friends these days. I wish
  some people I know would make them so!
  That's a joke.

TITANIA: You are beautiful, and you are wise.

BOTTOM: If I found a way to get out of this
wood, I'd be wise enough.

TITANIA: Do not wish to leave this wood.
You will stay here whether you wish or not.
I am like no one you have ever known.
The summer is a servant to my power,
And I do love you. So then, go with me.
I'll give you fairies who will wait on you.
They will bring you jewels from the sea
And sing you to sleep on beds of flowers.
I will take away your mortal grossness,
And you shall be as someone made of air.
Peaseblossom, Cobweb, Mote, and
Mustardseed!

(*Four* FAIRIES *enter:* PEASEBLOSSOM, COBWEB, MOTE,
and MUSTARDSEED.)

FAIRIES: Ready! Where shall we go?

TITANIA: Be kind to this gentleman.
Hop before him. Jump about in his sight.
Feed him with the finest fruits and honey.
For candles, use wax from the legs of bees.
Light them on a glow-worm's fiery eyes.
Let them show my love his way to bed.
Use the wings of painted butterflies
As fans to wake him softly. Serve him well.

PEASEBLOSSOM: Hail, mortal!

OTHER FAIRIES: Hail!

BOTTOM: Sirs, I cry your mercy. I hope I get to
know you all. Master Cobweb? Happy to
meet you, sir. If I cut my finger, I will need

you. Master Peaseblossom? My greetings to
your mother, Mrs. Pod, and your father,
Mr. Bean. And you, good Master Mustardseed,
I know you well. I've eaten many of your
family with roast beef. I tell you, having to
do so brought tears to my eyes! Happy to
know you, Master Mustardseed!

TITANIA: Wait on him. Lead him to my chambers.
Tie up my love's tongue. Bring him quietly.

(*They exit.*)

Scene 2

Another part of the wood. OBERON *enters.*

OBERON: I wonder if Titania's awake?
If so, I wonder what came to her eyes,
And now must be her dearest love?
(PUCK *enters.*)
Here is my messenger. How now, mad spirit?
What confusion did you bring to this wood?

PUCK: Your lady is in love with a monster.
Very near her chambers, while she slept,
I heard voices. I saw a crew of patches,
Rude men from Athenian workshops.
They were meeting to rehearse a play
They mean to act on Theseus's wedding day.
One who was most stupid and loud
Was playing the part of Pyramus. He left
His scene and went into the bushes.
That was when I got my chance with him.
I set a donkey's head upon his shoulders.
When his Thisbe called him, he came out,

And his friends saw my work. They flew away
As ducks do when they see a hunter come
With a gun. They rose and quacked
And ran away, screaming, in all directions.
One of them fell again and again
In his wild flight. He shouted "Murder!"
And called for help from Athens.
Their sense was weak, and so their fear
    was strong.
They even thought the bushes grabbed at
    them!
I led them on in their wild, crazy fear,
And left changed Pyramus standing there.
That was when Titania woke up
And found herself in love with a donkey.

OBERON: This is better than I planned.
    But have you yet juiced the Athenian's eyes
    As I ordered you?

PUCK: Yes, that's done too.
    I found him asleep, the woman at his side.
    He must have seen her first when he awoke.

(*Enter* DEMETRIUS *and* HERMIA.)

OBERON: Hide yourself. Here is the Athenian.

PUCK: This is the woman, but not the man.

(PUCK *and* OBERON *step aside.*)

DEMETRIUS: Why are you so cruel? I love you.
    You should treat your worst enemy this way!

HERMIA: I've held you off kindly until now.

I fear that I have reason for much worse.
Have you killed Lysander in his sleep?
Have your shoes stood in his blood?
Then kill me, too.
The sun was not so true as he to me.
Would he have left me as I lay asleep?
I don't believe it. I'd sooner think that I
Could dig a hole right through the earth,
And let the moon shine through.
I think you murdered him.
Your face looks like a killer's.

DEMETRIUS: Your cruelty does cut me to the
    heart!
Yes, you're the murderer. Yet you do look
As bright as Venus shining in the sky.

HERMIA: What is this to Lysander? Where is he?
Oh, good Demetrius, please give him to me!

DEMETRIUS: I'd rather give his body to my dogs.

HERMIA: Out, dog! You push me past the edge
Of my patience. Have you killed him, then?
If so, you are not a man. Tell me! Did you kill
him in his sleep? Oh, you brave one!
A snake could do as much! A snake did it!

DEMETRIUS: You have no reason to say this.
I did not kill Lysander. As far as I know,
He is not dead.

HERMIA: Then tell me he is well.

DEMETRIUS: If I could, what would it get me?

HERMIA: This present: never to see me again.
I hope you never will, if he be dead
Or not. I hate the sight of you.

(HERMIA *exits.*)

DEMETRIUS: There's no point in following her
When she's like this. I'll rest a while.
Sadness grows heavier when one needs
sleep.
Sleep owes my sadness. I might make it pay,
By waiting for its offer. Here I'll stay.

(*He lies down and falls asleep.*)

OBERON (*to* PUCK): What have you done?
This is the wrong Athenian! You have put
The love-juice on some true love's eyes.
Because of you, true love's turned false,
And not false love turned true!

PUCK: It's just bad luck.
For every man who holds true to his love,
A million more break promise after promise.

OBERON: Go now, faster than the wind.
Make sure you find Helena of Athens.
You'll know her by her sick sighs of love.
Use some trick to make sure she comes here.
I'll charm his eyes when she is near.

PUCK: I go, I go, look how I go:
Faster than an arrow from a bow.

(PUCK *exits.* OBERON *puts the juice on* DEMETRIUS*'s eyes.*)

OBERON: Flower, marked with purple dye,
    When Cupid lets his arrow fly,
    Sink at once in this man's eye.
    When his true love happens by,
    Let her shine, all in his eye,
    As bright as Venus in the sky.

(PUCK *enters.*)

PUCK: Captain of our fairy band,
    Helena is here at hand.
    And the man, mistook by me,
    Begs her love, as you will see.
    Shall we watch them, he and she?
    Lord, what fools these mortals be!

(OBERON *and* PUCK *step aside.* LYSANDER *and*
HELENA *enter.*)

LYSANDER: Why do you say I'm making fun of you?
    No one ever cries when he makes fun.
    Look at me! When I promise love, I cry.
    How can this in me seem false to you?
    I wear the badge of love to prove it true.

HELENA: You make yourself more a liar
    With every word. That promise is Hermia's!
    Have you left her? You promise her and me.
    Your promises, held one against the other,
    Even out and add up to nothing.

LYSANDER: I had no sense when I gave her my
    love.

HELENA: You have none now, it seems to me!

LYSANDER: Demetrius loves Hermia, not you.

DEMETRIUS (*waking up*): Helena, my goddess!
    To what, my love, can I compare your
      eyes?
    And your lips, made perfectly for kissing!
    When you hold up your hand, I think of
      snow
    On mountains high. Oh, let me kiss it now!

HELENA: Oh, wickedness! Oh, how cruel it is
    To play this game against me for your fun!
    If you had any good in you at all,
    You would not hurt me so. I know you hate me,
    But must you two mock me, as well?
    If you were men, as you both look to be,
    You would not use a gentle lady so.
    You two, with your promises and praise!
    I know you both love Hermia.
    What a fine job, to make a joke of me!
    Such men you are, to make a woman cry!

LYSANDER: You are not kind, Demetrius.
    I know that you love Hermia. She is yours.
    Give up your love of Helena to me,
    For I love her and will until I die.

HELENA: What wasted breath from both of you!

DEMETRIUS: Lysander, keep your Hermia.
    If ever I did love her, that is past.
    My heart has only been a guest with her,
    And now it has come home to Helena.

LYSANDER: Helena, it is not so.

DEMETRIUS: Don't talk about what you don't
know.
You put yourself in danger with your words,
And may pay for them. Here comes your
love.

(HERMIA *enters.*)

HERMIA (*to* LYSANDER): Dark night takes power
from the eyes,
But makes the ears quick to understand.
I found you not with my eyes, Lysander,
But with my ears. Why did you leave me?

LYSANDER: Why should I stay, when love is
pushing me?

HERMIA: What love could push Lysander from
my side?

LYSANDER: My love for Helena, who makes the night
More bright than all the stars.
Why did you come here? Surely you must know
I left you there because I hate you so?

HERMIA: You do not mean this. No, it can't be true.

HELENA: She is part of it, too! Now I know!
These three together, simply to be mean,
Have planned this little game. You, Hermia,
Whom I have called my sister! You do this?
Is this what all the secrets we have shared
Have come to? The many hours we spent
Feeling sad that time was hurrying by
And parting us—is this all forgotten?

Once we, two bodies, shared a single heart.
We were two birds who sang a single song,
Two lovely berries on a single stem.
Now will you tear all that we had apart?
Will you join with men in scorning me?
It is not kind; not how girls must be.
All women would join me in saying so.

HERMIA: Your words surprise me.
I do not scorn you. It seems you scorn me.

HELENA: Did you not send Lysander after me
To say he loves me? And Demetrius,
Your other love, who ran away from me
This very night? It wasn't you who told
him
To call me goddess? Why does he say this
To one he hates? Why, too, does Lysander
Say he does not love you?
Why does he cry out his love for me?
Was it not you who put him up to it?
I may not be as beautiful as you are.
I may not be as lucky as you are,
So hung upon with love. But one like me,
Most miserable, loving but not loved—
You should be kind to me, not hurt me so.

HERMIA: I do not understand what you mean.

HELENA: Yes, go on. Keep up your sad looks.
Make faces at me when I turn my back.
Wink at each other. Keep up your nice joke.

It will be written down in history.
If you were human beings at all,
You would not be doing this to me.
Good-bye. It's partly my own fault,
And I'll make up for it by leaving here.

LYSANDER: Stay, my Helena, my love, my life.

HERMIA (*to* LYSANDER): Dear, do not scorn her so.

DEMETRIUS (*to* LYSANDER): If *she* can't beg you,
I can make you stop.

LYSANDER: No you can't, no more than she can.
Your threats are as empty as her prayers.
Helena, I love you. By my life I do.

DEMETRIUS: I say I love you more than he can.

LYSANDER: If you say so, prove it.

HERMIA (*Taking hold of* LYSANDER): Lysander,
What is the point of all this?

LYSANDER: Away, you monkey! Let go of me,
Or I will shake you off me like a bug!

HERMIA: Why are you doing this?
What has changed you, sweet love?

LYSANDER: I, your love? You ugly thing!

HERMIA: You must be joking.

HELENA: Yes, and so are you.

LYSANDER: Demetrius, I'll keep my word.

DEMETRIUS: I wish I had it written down.
I do not trust your word.

HERMIA (*to* LYSANDER): Love, what is this?
Aren't I Hermia? Aren't you Lysander?
I am the same now as a while ago.
Last night you loved me. Why did you leave?
The gods forbid!—Could you be serious?

LYSANDER: Yes, by my life.
I never want to see you again.
Be sure. There's nothing truer. It's no joke
That I do hate you and love Helena.

HERMIA: Oh, me! (*She lets him go. To* HELENA)
You sneak! You worm! You thief!
You came by night and took my love from me!

HELENA: Have you no shame?
You would make me answer you in anger?
Go to the devil, you fake, you puppet!

HERMIA: "Puppet?" So that is how it goes!
I see now that she has won him over
By pointing out to him how tall she is.
And have you for Lysander grown so high
Because I am so short? How low am I?
How low am I, you painted maypole? Speak!
How low am I? I am not so short
That my nails cannot reach up to your eyes!

HELENA: Gentlemen, don't let her hurt me.
I have no heart for fighting, as does she.
I am a lady, indeed. Please do not think
Because she is something lower than myself
That I can match her.

HERMIA: "Lower?" Listen to her!

HELENA: Hermia, I never meant you wrong.
    I only told Demetrius, out of love,
    About your plan to come to this wood.
    He followed you for love. I followed him,
    But he drove me away. Now, let me go.
    Let me go back quietly to Athens
    And follow you no more. That's all I want.

HERMIA: Then go away. What keeps you here?

HELENA: A foolish heart, which I now leave behind.

HERMIA: What, with Lysander?

HELENA: With Demetrius.

LYSANDER: Don't be afraid. She shall not hurt
    you, Helena.

HELENA: Oh, when she is angry, she is nasty!
    She was a vixen when we were in school,
    She may be small, but she is tough.

HERMIA: "Small" again! Nothing but "low" and
        "small?"
    Why do you let her say this? Let me at her!

LYSANDER (*holding* HERMIA *back*): Away, you
    dwarf, you mouse, you ant, you acorn—

DEMETRIUS: You are too nice to Helena,
    And she does not want you. Let her be.
    Do not take her side. For if you make
    The smallest show of love for her,
    You'll pay for it.

LYSANDER: No one is holding me now.
Follow me, if you dare, and we will see
Which of us has more right to Helena.

DEMETRIUS: "Follow?" I'll go with you, toe to toe!

(LYSANDER *and* DEMETRIUS *exit.*)

HERMIA: You, friend, all this is your fault.
(HELENA *backs away.*) No, don't go back.

HELENA: I do not trust you. I won't stay.
Your hands may be quicker for a fight.
My legs are longer, though, to run away.

(HELENA *exits.*)

HERMIA: This is crazy. I don't know what to
make of it.

(HERMIA *exits.*)

OBERON (*to* PUCK): This is your doing.
Are you still making mistakes?
Or do you do such things on purpose?

PUCK: Believe me, my king, it's a mistake.
Didn't you tell me I would know the man
By the Athenian clothes he had on?
And didn't I follow your directions?
But so far I am glad that it was done,
For I find watching them to be great fun.

OBERON: Those men look for a place to fight.
Hurry, Puck, go make black the night.

Make them lose themselves in such a fog
That they can't do each other any harm.
Talk to them, each in the other's voice.
Talk like Lysander, and stir up Demetrius.
Then sometimes bellow like Demetrius.
Let them grow tired with their empty anger.
Wait until they fall in deathlike sleep,
And crush this flower in Lysander's eye.
(*He gives* PUCK *the flower.*)
It has the power to undo mistakes.
Make his eyes see as they used to see.
When they next awake, all their angry words
Will be a dream to them. The four of them
Will make their way back home to Athens.
They'll always feel united by this night.
While you do this, I'll go see my queen.
I'll ask her to please give the boy to me,
And from her donkey love, I'll set her free.

PUCK: My king, this must be done quickly.
The night is almost gone, the morning near.
Ghosts that haunt the dark are going home.
Already they do seek their wormy beds.
They keep themselves hidden from the day
And only go about by blackest night.

OBERON: But we are spirits of another kind.
I have often played and danced with dawn.
I've seen the sun come up, all fiery red.
But even so, you're right. Do not delay.
We may still finish with this before day.

(OBERON *exits.*)

46

PUCK: Up and down, up and down.
　　I will lead them up and down.
　　I am feared in field and town.
　　Goblin, lead them up and down.
　　Here comes one.

(LYSANDER *enters*.)

LYSANDER: Where are you, Demetrius?

PUCK (*in* DEMETRIUS*'s voice*): Here, pig.
　　My sword is ready.
　　Where are you?

LYSANDER: I'll be right there.

PUCK (*in* DEMETRIUS*'s voice*): Follow me, then,
　　To flatter ground.

(LYSANDER *exits*. DEMETRIUS *enters*.)

DEMETRIUS: Talk again, Lysander.
　　Have you run away, you coward? Talk!
　　Are you hiding in the bushes?

PUCK (*in* LYSANDER*'s voice*): Coward, you are
　　Bragging to the stars.
　　Tell the bushes that you want to fight.
　　Come, child. I would be ashamed
　　To fight you like a man. Follow my voice.

DEMETRIUS: Lysander, are you there?

(DEMETRIUS *and* PUCK *exit*. LYSANDER *enters*.)

LYSANDER: He runs, and still he dares me on.
　　I follow him, but then I find him gone.
　　He is too fast. Now I have lost my way.

I'll rest here. Come now, gentle day.
If only once you show me your gray light,
I'll find Demetrius and make him fight.

(LYSANDER *lies down and sleeps.* PUCK *and*
DEMETRIUS *enter.*)

PUCK (*in* LYSANDER*'s voice*): Ho, ho, ho!
Coward, why don't you show yourself?

DEMETRIUS: No, you're playing with me.
You'll pay for this
When I next see you by the light of day.
I'm tired. I must lie down on this cold bed
And wait for day to come.

(DEMETRIUS *lies down and sleeps.* HELENA *enters.*)

HELENA: Long night, cut short your hours!
Shine, sun! Let me get back to Athens,
Away from people who can't stand my sight.
Sleep, take me a while from my own company.

(HELENA *lies down and sleeps.* HERMIA *enters.*)

HERMIA: Never so tired, never so sad.
Wet from the night air, my clothes torn,
I can go no further. Here I will rest.
Heaven help Lysander if they fight.

(HERMIA *lies down and sleeps.*)

PUCK: On the ground,
Sleep sound.
I'll apply
This to your eye.
(*He puts the juice on* LYSANDER*'s eyes.*)

When you wake you will take
True delight in the sight
Of your true love's eye.
And a saying that is well known—
That every man should have his own—
In your waking shall be shown:
Jack shall have Jill, nothing will go ill.
The man shall have his mare again,
And all shall be well.

(PUCK *exits.*)

Act 4

Bottom is waited on by Titania while Oberon watches. They fall asleep. When Puck returns, Oberon has him break the spell. But Puck does not remove the donkey's head until Titania sees just what it is that she has loved. She and Oberon end their quarrel.

Theseus, Hippolyta, and Egeus are out celebrating May Day. They find the four young people asleep. Egeus is angry that Hermia and Lysander ran away together. But when Theseus sees how happy both couples are, he declares that they will be married the next day. Bottom, too, awakes and thinks he has been dreaming. His friends find him just in time for their play.

Scene 1

The wood. The four lovers are still asleep on stage. TITANIA *and* BOTTOM *enter, with* PEASEBLOSSOM, COBWEB, MOTE, *and* MUSTARDSEED. OBERON *enters behind the others, unseen by them.*

TITANIA: Come, sit upon these flowers fair.
   I will touch your lovely face
   And put wild roses in your hair.

BOTTOM: Where's Peaseblossom?

PEASEBLOSSOM: Ready.

BOTTOM: Scratch my head, Peaseblossom.
   Where's Mr. Cobweb?

COBWEB: Ready.

BOTTOM: Mr. Cobweb, get your bow and arrow. Kill me a bee and bring me the honeybag. Don't worry too much about it, and be careful not to break the honeybag. I'd hate to see you neck-deep in honey, good sir. *(COBWEB exits.)* Where's Mr. Mustardseed?

MUSTARDSEED: Ready.

BOTTOM: Lend me your hand, Mr. Mustardseed. And please, good sir, stop bowing.

MUSTARDSEED: What do you wish?

BOTTOM: Just a scratch. I must find a barber, sir. I seem to have grown a lot of hair on my face. I am such a tender donkey. If my hair tickles me, I must scratch.

TITANIA: Would you like some music, my love?

BOTTOM: I have a good ear for music. Let us have the spoons and the bones.

TITANIA: Or, sweet love, maybe you would like Something fine to eat?

BOTTOM: A bag of hay, or maybe some oats. Good, sweet hay, there's nothing like it.

TITANIA: One of my fairies will get for you Fresh nuts from a squirrel's den.

BOTTOM: I'd rather have some dried peas. But, I ask you, have none of your people disturb me. All at twice I'm very sleepy.

TITANIA: Sleep, then. I will wind you in my arms. Fairies, be gone. *(The FAIRIES exit.)*

As does the female ivy circle 'round
An elm tree's barky fingers. I love you!
Oh, how I love you!

(BOTTOM *and* TITANIA *sleep.* PUCK *enters.*)

OBERON: Look at this sweet sight.
I now begin to pity her blind love.
I met her in the wood a while ago,
Seeking sweet favors for this ugly fool.
I argued with her, and I scolded her.
For she had put a crown of flowers
Around his hairy head. And beads of dew
Shone in those pretty little flowers' eyes,
Like tears cried in their own disgrace.
When I had finished saying what I thought,
She begged me softly not to tease her so.
That was when I asked her for the child.
She gave him up at once. She told a fairy
To send him to my chamber in Fairyland.
Now that I have the boy, I will undo
The magic that I placed upon her eyes.
And, gentle Puck, take the donkey's head
Off the head of this Athenian.
Let him awake when the others do.
Let them all go home to Athens now.
Let them think this night was just a dream.
But first I will set free the fairy queen.
(He puts the juice on TITANIA*'s eyes.)*
Be now as you used to be.
See now as you used to see.
This sweet bud shall have the power

To end the work of Cupid's flower.
Now, my Titania, my sweet queen, awake.

TITANIA *(waking)*: Oberon, what dreams I had!
I thought I was in love with a donkey!

OBERON: There lies your love.

TITANIA: How did these things happen?
Oh, how my eyes do hate the sight of him!

OBERON: Quiet now. Puck, take off his head.
Titania, call for music. As for these five,
Let them think they've slept all night.

TITANIA: Give us music to charm their sleep.

(PUCK *removes the donkey's head from* BOTTOM.)

OBERON: Play, music. Come, my queen, join
hands with me,
And rock the ground on which these
sleepers be.
(Music plays. TITANIA *and* OBERON *dance.)*
Now you and I are friends again, and we
Will dance secretly tomorrow night
In Theseus's house. There we will see
That these two pairs of lovers, happily
Will, with duke and duchess, married be.

PUCK: Fairy king, listen and hear.
A bird tells me that morning's near.

OBERON: Then, my queen, let us take flight
Quickly now and follow night.

TITANIA: Come, my husband. As we go,
Tell me how it happened so.

How was it, please, that I was found
Asleep with mortals on the ground?

(OBERON, TITANIA, *and* PUCK *exit. A horn sounds.*
THESEUS, *his* SERVANTS, HIPPOLYTA, *and* EGEUS *enter.*)

THESEUS: Go, one of you. Find the man
Who looks after the forest and its animals.
We have finished with the May Day rite.
And, as it is still early, we may hunt.
My love shall hear the music of my dogs.
Let them loose in the western valley.
Go, I say, and find the forest keeper.
(*A* SERVANT *exits.*)
We will go, love, to the mountain's top.
There we will listen to the wild music
Of hounds and their echo joined together.

HIPPOLYTA: I was hunting once with Hercules.
We were after bear in a wood of Crete,
With hounds of Spartan breed. I never heard
Such stirring sounds. For all the trees,
The sky, the water, seemed to cry as one.
So musical a noise! Such sweet thunder!

THESEUS: My dogs are also of that kind:
Sand-colored, large folds around the mouth.
Their fine ears sweep away the morning dew.
Slow, yes, but voices matched like bells,
Each tuned to each. A cry more musical
Was never heard by any hunter's ears.
Judge when you hear. But wait! Who is this?

EGEUS: My lord, this is my daughter.
And here is Lysander, and here Demetrius.

And this is Helena, old Nedar's daughter.
I wonder what they're doing here together.

THESEUS: I'm sure they got up early to take part
In the May Day rite. They must have heard
That we were planning to observe it here
And wanted to be with us.
But speak, Egeus. Isn't this the day
That Hermia must tell you of her choice?

EGEUS: It is, my lord.

THESEUS: Go, have the hunters wake them with
their horns.
(*A* SERVANT *exits. A shout from offstage. Horns
sound. The four lovers start to wake up.*)
Good morning, friends. Valentine's is past.
Do these birds only start to pair off now?

(DEMETRIUS, HELENA, HERMIA, *and* LYSANDER *kneel.*)

LYSANDER: Pardon, my lord.

THESEUS. Please, all of you, stand up.
(*They rise.*)
I know you four are not the best of friends.
How, with your feelings for each other, can
You sleep so close together without fear?

LYSANDER: My lord, I am still half asleep.
I am amazed. I cannot truly say
How I came here. But I will tell the truth.
And now that I remember, it is this:
I came here with Hermia. We planned
To run away from Athens, and be free
Of Athenian law—

EGEUS: Enough! My lord, you've heard enough!
 I beg you, bring the law upon his head.
 Demetrius, they would have run away.
 They would have robbed you of your wife
 And me of my rights as a father.

DEMETRIUS: My lord, Helena told me their plan.
 I followed them in anger, and fair Helena,
 Drawn by love, followed me. But, my lord,
 By some power, my love for Hermia
 Melted like snow. It seems now like a toy
 I treasured as a child. Now all my love
 Belongs to Helena. She is the strength
 Of my heart, and the pleasure of my eye.
 Now I want her, love her, long for her,
 And I will be forever true to her.

THESEUS: Lovers, you are lucky we found you.
 Egeus, I must rule against your will.
 These two couples will be married soon.
 Let them stand beside us in the temple.
 And now that the morning is flying by,
 We'll set aside our hunting. Come with us
 Back to Athens, all of you. Three by three,
 The feast we'll hold will live in memory.
 Come, Hippolyta.

(THESEUS, *his* SERVANTS, HIPPOLYTA, *and* EGEUS *exit.*)

DEMETRIUS: These things seem small now,
 Like far-off mountains that are only clouds.

HERMIA: I see them with a sleepy eye,
 And everything seems double.

HELENA: To me, too.
And I have found Demetrius, like a jewel
That is not mine to own.

DEMETRIUS: Are you sure we are awake?
It seems to me that we are still dreaming.
Was the duke just here?

HERMIA: Yes, and my father.

HELENA: And Hippolyta.

LYSANDER: And Theseus wants us to follow to
the temple.

DEMETRIUS: Why then, we are awake. Let's go,
And on the way, let us tell our dreams.

(*The four lovers exit.*)

BOTTOM (*waking up*): Call me when my next cue
comes. I will answer. It is "Most fair
Pyramus." Hello? Peter Quince? Flute?
Snout, the tinker? Starveling? God's my life!
Stolen here and left asleep! I have had a
most rare dream. I have had a dream past
the sense of any man to say what dream it
was. Man is but a donkey if he thinks he can
explain this dream. I thought I was—no man
can tell what. I thought I was—I thought I
had—Any man is a fool who tries to say
what I thought I had. The eye of man has
not heard it. The ear of man cannot see it.
Man's hand is not able to taste it. His
tongue is not able to hold or his heart to

say what my dream was. I will get Peter Quince to write a song about it. It will be called "Bottom's Dream" because it has no bottom. I will sing it toward the end of a play, before the duke. (*He exits.*)

Scene 2

Peter Quince's house. QUINCE, FLUTE, SNOUT, *and* STARVELING *enter.*

QUINCE: Have you been to Bottom's house? Has he come home yet?

STARVELING: He has not come. No doubt something has happened to him.

FLUTE: If he doesn't show up, our play is ruined. It can't go on, can it?

QUINCE: It is not possible. There is no other man in Athens who can play Pyramus.

FLUTE: No, he is the smartest working man in Athens.

QUINCE: Yes, and the best-looking, too. And he has the sweetest voice.

(SNUG *enters.*)

SNUG: Masters, the duke is coming from the temple, with more lords and ladies who were just married. If our play had gone on, we would have had it made.

FLUTE: Oh, Bottom! He just lost sixpence a day for the rest of his life. He could not have escaped it. If the duke would have given him that much for playing Pyramus, he would have deserved it.

(BOTTOM *enters*.)

BOTTOM: Where are my good fellows?

QUINCE: Bottom! Oh, great day!

BOTTOM: Masters, I have wonders to tell you. But don't ask me to! If I tell you, I am not a true Athenian. I will tell you everything right as it fell out.

QUINCE: Let us hear, sweet Bottom.

BOTTOM: Not a word from me. All I will tell you is that the duke has had his dinner. Get your costumes together, and strings to tie on your beards. Meet at the palace. Every man read over his part. Let Thisbe wear clean clothes. And lion, don't cut your nails. Let them hang out for claws. And, dear actors, eat no onions or garlic. This is a sweet comedy, and we must have sweet breath. No more words. Away!

(*They exit.*)

Act 5

The newly married couples are at Theseus's palace. Theseus is amused by the four lovers' stories of what has happened. He is sure they dreamed the whole thing. Bottom and his friends perform their play for the duke and his guests. When it is over and everyone has gone to bed, the fairies slip into the palace. Oberon and Titania bless the three marriages, but it is Puck who has the last word.

Scene 1

Theseus's palace. THESEUS, HIPPOLYTA, PHILOSTRATE, GUESTS, *and* SERVANTS *enter.*

HIPPOLYTA: These lovers tell a strange story, my
    Theseus.

THESEUS: More strange than true.
    I don't believe in fairy tales.
    Lovers' brains boil over. Their fantasies
    Are more than cool sense ever understands.
    The insane, the lover, and the poet
    Are made of nothing but imagination.
    One who sees more devils than hell can hold:
    That is the madman. The lover, just as mad,
    Sees great beauty in the plainest face.
    The poet's eye rolls from heaven to earth,
    And back again. His imagination
    Brings forth unknown things, and his pen
    Turns them into shapes with homes and
        names.
    Imagination plays such tricks! If you

Imagine joy, then there has to be
A bringer of that joy.
Or in the night, if you imagine fear,
A bush can easily seem to be a bear!

HIPPOLYTA: But their stories are so alike.
Their minds are shaped to the same fantasy.
It seems like more than just imagination.
In any case, it's to be wondered at.

(LYSANDER, HERMIA, DEMETRIUS, *and* HELENA *enter.*)

THESEUS: Here come the happy lovers.
Joy, gentle friends!
Joy and fresh days of love to all of you!

LYSANDER: More to you than to us!

THESEUS: Come now, what plays and dances
Shall we have for entertainment?
Come, Philostrate, tell us.

(PHILOSTRATE *comes forward and gives* THESEUS *a paper.*)

PHILOSTRATE: Here, mighty Theseus. This is a list
Of all who are ready here this evening
To bring you joy with music or with wit.

THESEUS: "A tedious, short scene of Pyramus
and his love Thisbe, very sad comedy."
"Comedy" and "sad?" "Tedious" and "short?"
This is hot ice! What do they mean by this?

PHILOSTRATE: My lord, if this play were
Only ten words long,
It would be too long by those ten words.
That makes it tedious. As for sad, it is,
For at the end Pyramus kills himself.

And I did cry when I saw it rehearsed,
But my tears came from laughter.

THESEUS: Who are they who play it?

PHILOSTRATE: Hard-handed working men
Who never labored with their minds before.
They worked on this play for your wedding.

THESEUS: And we shall hear it.
For nothing can be wrong if it is done
With sincere good wishes. Send them in.
Gentlemen and ladies, take your places.

(PHILOSTRATE *exits.*)

HIPPOLYTA: I hate to see people embarrass
themselves
And kill good wishes with bad efforts.

THESEUS: Dear, you will see no such thing.
Let us be kind and show these men respect.
I have been greeted by men of learning
Who meant to welcome me with pretty talk
But dropped their words in fear. Trust me,
my love.
I could hear welcome in their silence
As much as from others' rattling tongues.
Good wishes say a great deal to me.

(PHILOSTRATE *enters.*)

PHILOSTRATE: Sir, they are ready.

THESEUS: Let them begin.

(QUINCE, BOTTOM, FLUTE, SNOUT, SNUG, *and*
STARVELING *enter.*)

QUINCE *(reciting Prologue)*: If we offend, it is
    with our good wishes.
  Do not think we come here to offend,
  But with good wishes. To do our play
  Is the true beginning of our end.
  Don't think we come only to trouble you.
  We do not come, as minding to please you.
  Our true wish is. All for your delight
  We are not here. That you should feel sorry
  The actors are all here. And by our show,
  You shall know all that you want to know.

THESEUS: This fellow does not know what a
    sentence is.

LYSANDER: He says his lines like a colt:
  He does not know where to stop.

HIPPOLYTA: He talks like a child plays the flute:
  With sound, but no sense.

Quince *(reciting Prologue)*: You all may wonder
    at our show.
  Well, wonder on until we make things plain.
  This man is Pyramus, if you must know.
  This beautiful lady is Thisbe for certain.
  This is the Wall, through which these two
  Had to whisper their words of love so true.
  This man is Moonlight. You must know
  They meet by night at Ninus's tomb to woo.
  This is the Lion that scared Thisbe away.
  And, as she ran, her coat fell by the way.
  The Lion chewed it with its bloody mouth.

When Pyramus came by, with his tall head,
He found that sweet Thisbe's coat was dead.
With a blade, he burst his burning breast.
And Thisbe, waiting nearby in the shade
Drew his dagger, and died. For the rest,
Let Lion, Moonlight, Wall and lovers two
Tell you the story, until they are through.

THESEUS: I wonder if the Lion will talk.

DEMETRIUS: I won't be surprised.
One lion may talk, if many donkeys do.

SNOUT *(as Wall)*: In this play, I, Snout,
Do play a Wall. In this Wall is a hole
Through which our Pyramus and Thisbe
Did whisper often, very secretly.
This plaster and this stone do show
That I am that same Wall. The truth is so.

THESEUS: Could stone speak any better?

DEMETRIUS: It is the most well-spoken wall
I have ever heard, sir.

BOTTOM *(as Pyramus)*: Oh, darkest night! Oh,
night so black!
Oh night, which always is when day is not!
I fear my Thisbe's promise is forgot.
And you, oh Wall, oh sweet, lovely Wall,
You stand between her father's land and me.
Show me a hole to look through with my eye.
Thanks, Wall. Live and be well for this.
But what is this? No Thisbe do I see.
Oh, curse you, evil Wall, for lying to me!

THESEUS: If Wall can talk, I think he should curse back.

BOTTOM: No, truly, sir, he should not. Thisbe must enter now, and I will see her through the hole. Here she comes.

FLUTE *(as Thisbe)*: Oh Wall, often you have heard me cry for separating Pyramus and me.
My lips have so often kissed these stones.

BOTTOM *(as Pyramus)*: I see a voice!
Now let me hear my love's face!

FLUTE *(as Thisbe)*: My love! You are my love, I think.

BOTTOM *(as Pyramus)*: Think what you will, Like the dearest love, I am trusty still.

FLUTE *(as Thisbe)*: And I too, until the gods do kill!

BOTTOM *(as Pyramus)*: Oh, kiss me through the hole of this vile Wall.

FLUTE *(as Thisbe)*: I kiss the Wall, and not your lips at all.

BOTTOM *(as Pyramus)*: Will you meet me tonight at Ninny's tomb?

FLUTE *(as Thisbe)*: Alive or dead, I will meet you there soon.

(BOTTOM *and* FLUTE *exit.*)

SNOUT *(as Wall)*: Now I have played my part just so,
And, being done, the Wall away does go.

(SNOUT *exits.*)

HIPPOLYTA: This is the silliest play I have ever
    seen.

THESEUS: The best actors are only shadows.
    The worst are no worse, if imagination
    makes them better.

HIPPOLYTA: It must be your imagination, then,
    and not theirs.

THESEUS: Let us imagine no worse of them
    Than they of themselves. That will make
    them very fine men.

SNUG *(as Lion)*: Ladies, your hearts fear
    The smallest mouse upon the floor.
    You may well scream out here,
    When you hear a lion roar.
    Know that I, Snug, the joiner am.
    I am no lion, just a man.

THESEUS: A very kind and gentle animal.

DEMETRIUS: The very best beast I ever saw.

STARVELING *(as Moonlight)*: This lantern is to be
    the moon,
    And I am to be seen as the Man in the Moon.

THESEUS: This is a big mistake. Shouldn't the
    man then be inside the lantern?

DEMETRIUS: He must be afraid of the candle.

HIPPOLYTA: I am tired of the moon. I wish he
    would set.

THESEUS: Indeed, he seems rather dim.
    We must wait for him to fade away.

DEMETRIUS: Quiet. Here comes Thisbe.

(FLUTE *enters*.)

FLUTE *(as Thisbe)*: This is old Ninny's tomb.
Where is my love?

SNUG *(as Lion)*: Roar!

(FLUTE *as Thisbe runs off, dropping her coat.*
SNUG *as Lion tears at it with his teeth.*)

DEMETRIUS: Well roared, Lion.

THESEUS: Well run, Thisbe.

HIPPOLYTA: Well shone, Moon.

THESEUS: Well torn, Lion.

(BOTTOM *enters.* SNUG *exits.*)

BOTTOM *(as Pyramus)*: Sweet Moon, I thank you
For your sunny light.
I thank you, Moon, for shining bright.
I trust it will bring Thisbe to my sight.
But wait! Oh, no! But look, just so!
What awful sadness is here!
Eyes, can you see? How can it be?
Oh, sweet duck! Oh, dear!
Your coat so good is stained with blood!
Come near, oh, terrible gods!
Cut the thread of my life!
Beat me, crush me, end me, kill me!

THESEUS: This strong feeling, and the death of a
dear friend, would almost make a man look
sad.

HIPPOLYTA: Curse my heart, but I pity him.

BOTTOM *(as Pyramus)*: Oh, Nature, why did you
make lions?
A lion has here eaten my dear!
She is—no, no—she was the fairest lady
That lived and loved and looked with cheer.
Come tears, destroy me!
Out, sword, and wound me!
Cut the left side of Pyramus
Where the heart hops.
(He pretends to stab himself.)
So I die, like so, like so.
Now I am dead; my blood is red.
My soul is in the sky.
Tongue, lose your light!
Moon, make your flight. (MOONLIGHT *exits.)*
Now die, die, die, die! (PYRAMUS *falls.)*

HIPPOLYTA: Why is Moonlight gone before Thisbe
comes back and finds him?

THESEUS: She will find him by the stars.
(FLUTE *enters, as Thisbe.)*
Here she comes. Her speech ends the play.

HIPPOLYTA: I hope it will be short. Such a
Pyramus does not deserve a long one.

LYSANDER: She has seen him already with those
sweet eyes.

DEMETRIUS: And so she cries, as follows:

FLUTE *(as Thisbe)*: Asleep, my love?
What, dead, my dove?
Oh, Pyramus, get up!
Speak, speak! Quite dumb?

Dead? Dead? A tomb
Must cover your sweet eyes.
Those white lips, that rose-red nose,
These yellow cheeks are gone!
Lovers, cry with me!
His eyes were green as green onions.
Oh, death, come to me
With your hands, white as milk.
Lay them in blood. Tongue, not a word!
Come, happy sword, cover me with red!
(She pretends to stab herself.)
Good-bye, friends. So Thisbe ends.
Good-bye, good-bye, good-bye. *(She falls.)*

THESEUS: Moonlight and Lion are left to bury the dead.

DEMETRIUS: Yes, and Wall too.

(BOTTOM *and* FLUTE *stand up.*)

BOTTOM: No, I promise you, their fathers have torn down the wall. Will it please you to see the Epilogue? Or would you like to hear our group dance?

THESEUS: No epilogue, please. Your play needs no excuse.
When the players are all dead, there is no one to blame.
If he that wrote it had played Pyramus and hanged himself
In Thisbe's stocking, that would have been a fine tragedy.
And so it is, and very well performed.
But, come, let's see your dance.

(The players dance, and exit.)
The iron tongue of midnight has rung 12.
Let's all go to bed. It's fairy time.
I fear we will sleep away the morning,
Because we have stayed up so late tonight.
This play goes well with night's slow pace.
Good night, my friends. Two weeks from now,
We'll all meet here for another feast.

(All exit. PUCK *enters.)*

PUCK: Now the hungry lion roars,
And the wolf howls at the moon.
Now the tired farmer snores,
With his heavy day's work done.
Now the fire's light burns low.
Now the night bird, with its cry,
Reminds the man who lies in woe
That someday he will have to die.
Now it is the time of night
For the graves to open wide.
Everyone lets out its sprite.
Through the dark streets they will glide.
And we fairies now will run
By the moonlight's shining beam.
We fly from the morning sun,
Following darkness like a dream.
This is our time. Not a mouse
Shall disturb this happy house.
And I am sent here with a broom
To sweep the dust from every room.

*(*OBERON *and* TITANIA *enter, with their* FAIRIES.*)*

OBERON: Through the house, give us light

From the dead and sleepy fire.
Every elf and fairy sprite
Hop as light as bird from brier.
Sing this song along with me.
Dance together—one, two, three!

TITANIA: Softly let the music float.
For each word, a birdlike note.
Hand in hand, with fairy grace,
We will sing and bless this place.

(OBERON *leads the* FAIRIES *in song and dance.*)

OBERON: Now, until the break of day,
Through this house we'll go our way.
We will visit every room
And bless every bride and groom.
So shall all the couples three
Ever true in loving be.
Bless the children that they make.
Never from them good luck take.
And their children's faces be
From ugly marks forever free.
Bless this palace through and through
With this magic fairy dew.
Every fairy through it race,
Bringing everyone sweet peace.
Dance away. Do not stay.
Meet me all by break of day.

(*All but* PUCK *exit.*)

PUCK: If we shadows have offended,
Just think this, and all is mended:
That you have been sleeping here

While these strange scenes did appear.
And our weak and silly theme
Means no more than just a dream.
Good people, do not hiss and boo.
Next time, we'll make it up to you.
And, as I am an honest Puck,
If somehow we've had the luck
To escape your angry tongue,
We'll deserve it before long.
Or else the Puck a liar call.
So we say good night to all.
Give me your hands, if we be friends,
And sweet Puck shall restore amends.

(*Puck exits.*)